NARWHAL'S

MONODON MONOCEROS

SCHOOL OF AWESOMENESS

BEN CLANTON

IN MEMORY OF THE KIND, CURIOUS AND CREATIVE
CROSLEY JAYNE BUCHNER

AND WITH MY THANKS TO PROF. AMADOU FOFANA, SUE BROWN, GLENDA SKEIM, PROF. JEANNE CLARK, PROF. JOYCE MILLEN, PROF. REBECCA DOBKINS, MIKE MCGARVEY, ALLEN SLATER, CINDY GALVIN AND ALL THE EDUCATORS WHO HAVE CHALLENGED AND INSPIRED ME. ALSO TO TEACHERS WHO HAVE HELPED MY BOOKS FIND READERS, ESPECIALLY MICHELE O'HARE!

Farshore

FIRST PUBLISHED IN CANADA 2021 BY TUNDRA BOOKS
FIRST PUBLISHED IN GREAT BRITAIN 2021 BY FARSHORE
AN IMPRINT OF HARPERCOLLINS*PUBLISHERS*
1 LONDON BRIDGE STREET, LONDON SE1 9GF

FARSHORE.CO.UK

HARPERCOLLINS*PUBLISHERS*
1ST FLOOR, WATERMARQUE BUILDING, RINGSEND ROAD
DUBLIN 4, IRELAND
TEXT AND ILLUSTRATIONS COPYRIGHT © BEN CLANTON 2021
THE AUTHOR AND ILLUSTRATOR HAVE ASSERTED THEIR MORAL RIGHTS.

PUBLISHED BY ARRANGEMENT WITH TUNDRA BOOKS, AN IMPRINT OF PENGUIN RANDOM HOUSE CANADA YOUNG READERS, A PENGUIN RANDOM HOUSE COMPANY

EDITED BY TARA WALKER AND PETER PHILLIPS
DESIGNED BY BEN CLANTON | COLOURING BY JAIME TEMAIRIK AND BEN CLANTON
THE ARTWORK IN THIS BOOK WAS RENDERED IN COLOURED PENCIL, WATERCOLOUR AND INK, AND COLOURED DIGITALLY.
THE TEXT WAS SET IN A TYPEFACE BASED ON HAND-LETTERING BY BEN CLANTON.

PHOTOS: (CHALKBOARD) © STUDIO DREAM/SHUTTERSTOCK; (STRAWBERRY) © VALENTINA RAZUMOVA/SHUTTERSTOCK; (WAFFLE) © TIGER IMAGES/SHUTTERSTOCK; (PINEAPPLE) © DAYSUPA/SHUTTERSTOCK; (FRIES) © DROZHZHINA ELENA/SHUTTERSTOCK; (SCALES) © NATALIA KUDRYAVTSEVA/SHUTTERSTOCK; (SCALES 2) © HPL17/SHUTTERSTOCK

ISBN 978 0 7555 0007 9

PRINTED AND BOUND IN ITALY

1

CONTENTS

ONE DAY WHEN NARWHAL AND JELLY
WERE BLOWING SOME BUBBLES . . .

HUH! THAT'S KIND OF
FISHY. I WONDER
WHERE ALL THOSE
FISH ARE GOING . . .

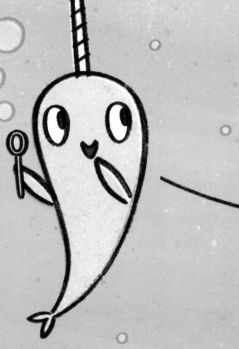

HMMM!
  MAYBE THEY'RE . . .

GOING TO A POOL PARTY!

POOL PARTY?! WHY WOULD THEY NEED A POOL? THEY'RE ALREADY IN THE WATER.

TRUE! THE SEA IS ONE BIG BEAUTIFUL COOL POOL!

OH! OR MAYBE THEY'RE GOING TO . . .

GIGGLE SWICK!

GIGGLESWICK?

GO AHEAD AND GIVE IT A GO, JELLY!

ME? HMMM... OKAY.

GIGGLESWICK!

HEY! THAT WAS FUN! BUT I DOUBT THAT'S WHERE THOSE FISH ARE GOING.

MAYBE THEY'RE GOING TO PLAY GO FISH!

OR LOOK FOR THE GREAT WHITE WHALE! OR –

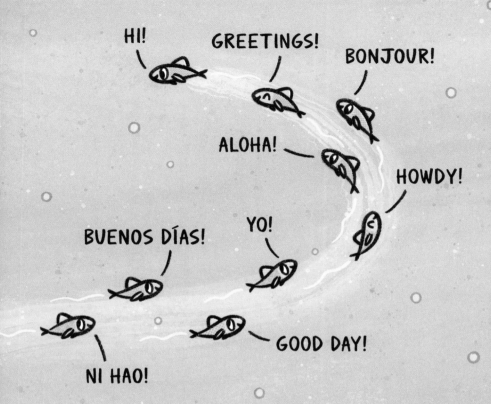

HI!

GREETINGS!

BONJOUR!

ALOHA!

HOWDY!

BUENOS DÍAS!

YO!

GOOD DAY!

NI HAO!

I'M NARWHAL THE NARWHAL!

UNICORN OF THE SEA!

UM . . . HI. I'M JELLY.

THE JELLYFISH.

THOSE ARE SOME FINTASTIC NAMES!

DEFINITELY!

WHERE ARE YOU ALL GOING?

SCHOOL!

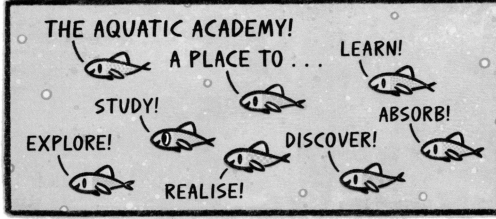

THE AQUATIC ACADEMY! A PLACE TO . . . LEARN!

STUDY!

ABSORB!

EXPLORE!

DISCOVER!

REALISE!

OOO! COOL! I WANT TO COME TOO!

LET'S GO!

MR. BLOWFISH!

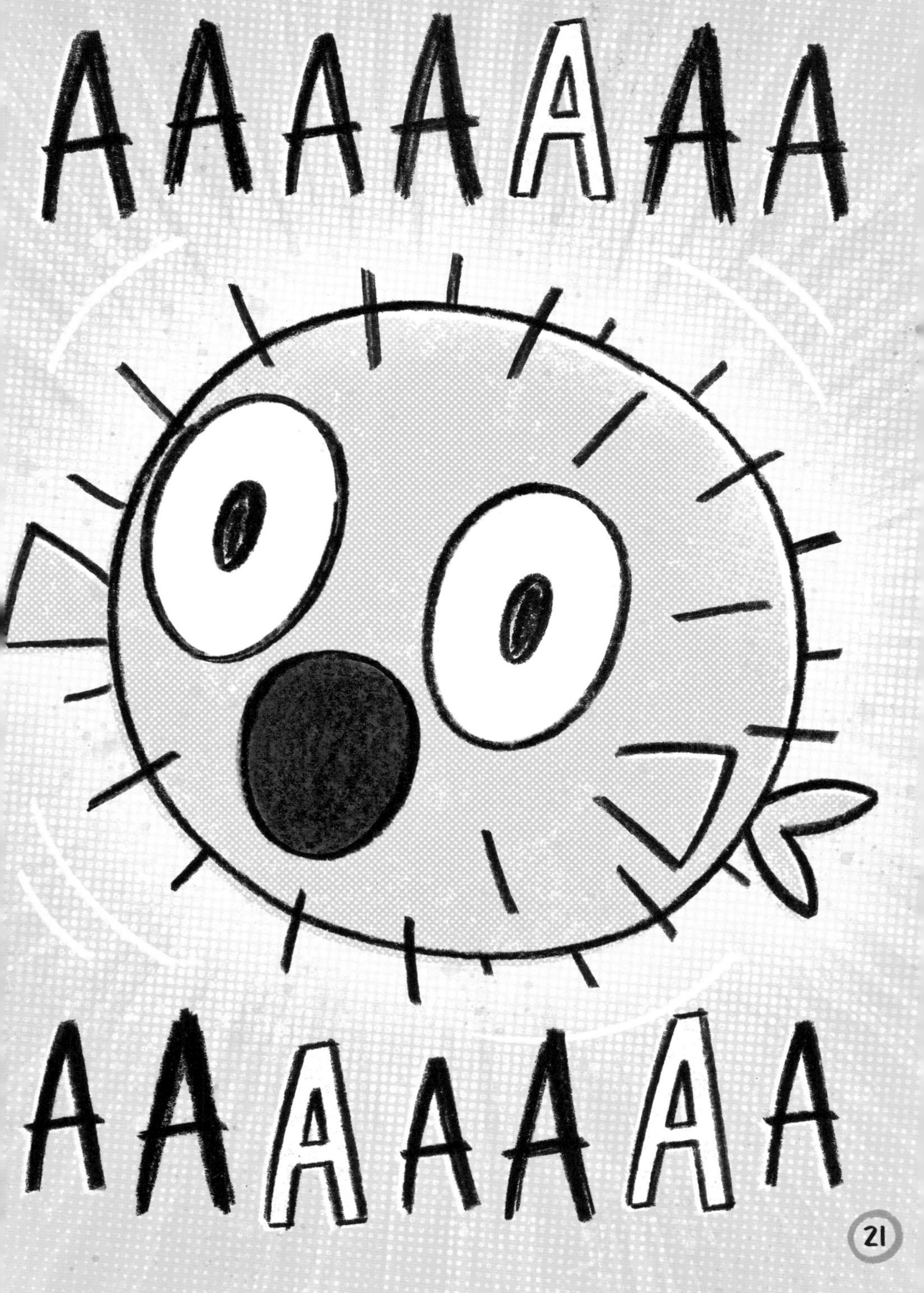
AAAAAAA
AAAAAAA

CHOOOOOOOOO

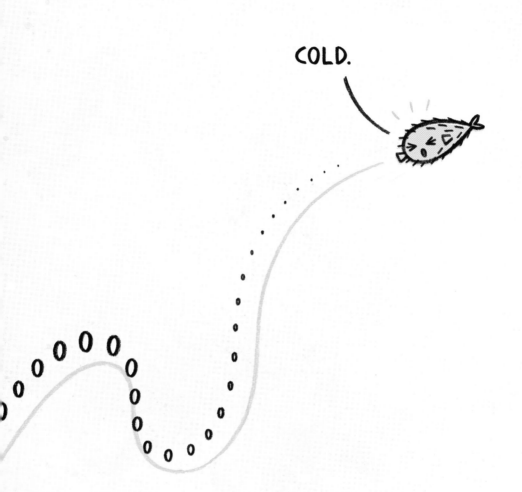

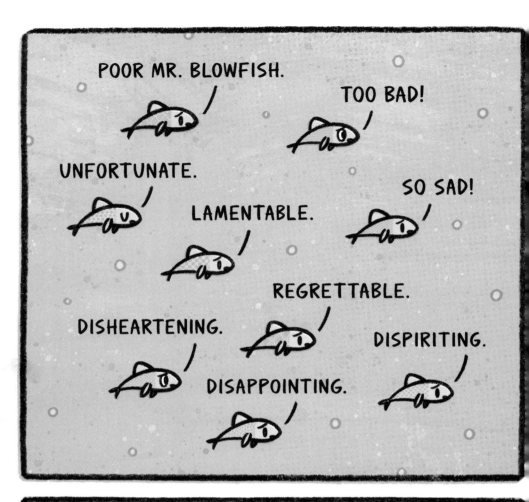

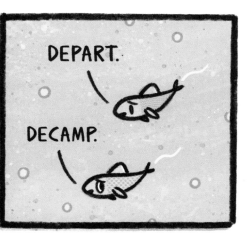

A SUPER TEACHER?

PRETTY MUCH!

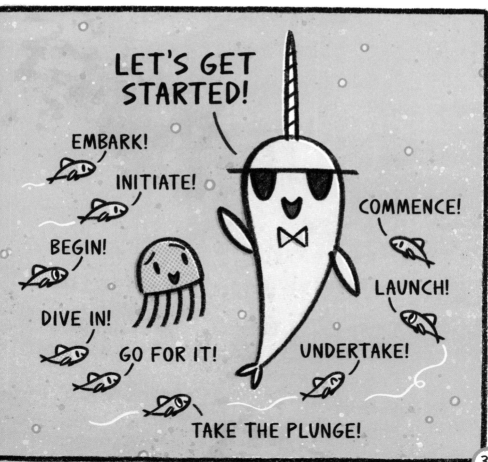

LET'S GET STARTED!

EMBARK!

INITIATE!

COMMENCE!

BEGIN!

LAUNCH!

DIVE IN!

GO FOR IT!

UNDERTAKE!

TAKE THE PLUNGE!

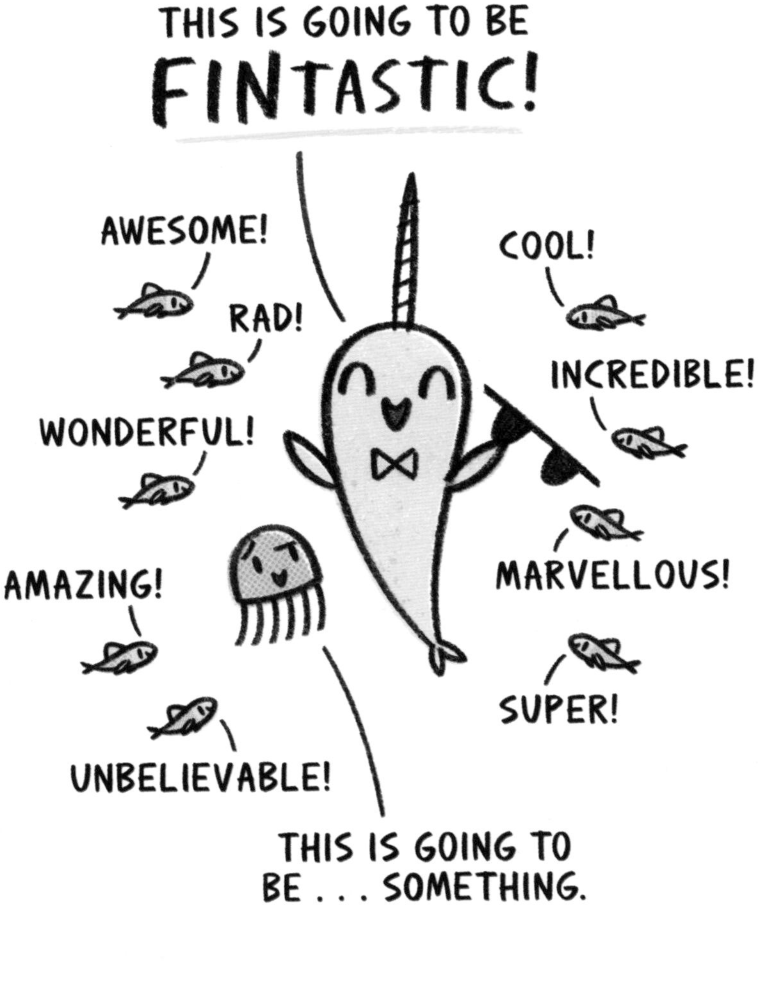
THIS IS GOING TO BE FINTASTIC!
AWESOME!
COOL!
RAD!
INCREDIBLE!
WONDERFUL!
MARVELLOUS!
AMAZING!
SUPER!
UNBELIEVABLE!
THIS IS GOING TO BE . . . SOMETHING.

A GREAT GROUP
OF FUN FACTS

YOU PROBABLY ALREADY KNOW THAT A GROUP OF CHICKENS IS CALLED A FLOCK AND A GROUP OF DEER IS COMMONLY CALLED A HERD. BUT HAVE YOU HEARD OF A TOWER OF GIRAFFES OR A BLOAT OF HIPPOS? MANY SEA CREATURES HAVE FUN GROUP NAMES TOO!

NEAT!

FASCINATING!

CAPTIVATING!

INTERESTING!

A GROUP OF FISH ALL THE SAME SPECIES AND SWIMMING IN SYNC IS KNOWN AS A SCHOOL. THE SIZE AND SYNCHRONISED MOVEMENTS OF A SCHOOL OF FISH CAN CONFUSE AND EVEN SCARE PREDATORS.

EEP! MONSTER!

MORE!
FURTHER!
OTHER!
EXTRA!

FUN FACTS

A GROUP OF SEA SNAILS IS CALLED A WALK.

HOW ABOUT A SPRINT?

OR RUN!

MAYBE A JOG OF SNAILS?

A GROUP OF OYSTERS IS CALLED A BED.

BUT YOU WOULDN'T WANT TO SLEEP ON US!

OW!

A GROUP OF SHARKS IS OFTEN CALLED A SHIVER.

YARGH! SHIVER ME TIMBERS!

WHERE BE ME CREW?!

SO WHAT'S TODAY'S FIRST SUBJECT, PROFESSOR KNOWELL?

HMMM, HOW ABOUT . . .

WAFFLES!

UHHH, YOU KNOW WAFFLES AREN'T AN ACTUAL SCHOOL SUBJECT, RIGHT?

OH! MAYBE THEY SHOULD BE!

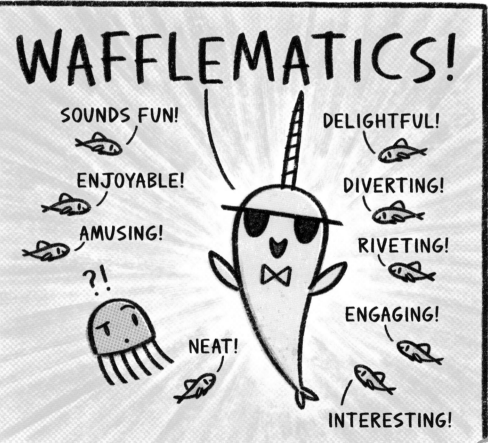

WAFFLEMATICS?!

IS THAT A REAL THING?

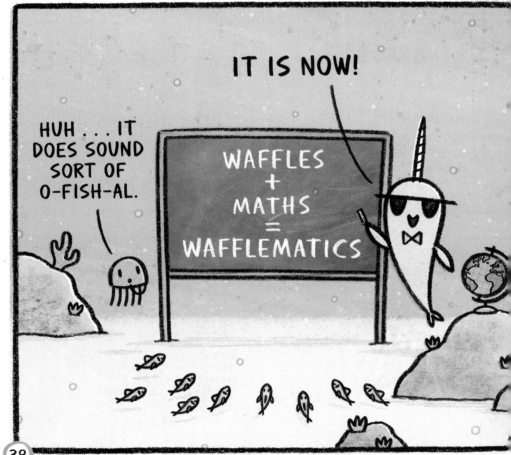

IT IS NOW!

HUH . . . IT DOES SOUND SORT OF O-FISH-AL.

WAFFLES
+
MATHS
=
WAFFLEMATICS

LET'S START WITH A SUPER IMPORTANT PROBLEM...

HOW MANY WAFFLES DO I NEED TO MAKE FOR US?

HMM...

LET'S COUNT.

STARTING WITH...

ONE!

TWO!

TRUE!
BUT I WANT
TO EAT AT
LEAST SEVEN
WAFFLES!

OH! I'D LIKE
TWO ACTUALLY!

ME TOO!

THREE FOR ME!

AND FOUR
FOR ME!

THIS IS WHAT I'M CHALKING
ABOUT! THIS IS ADDING UP
TO OODLES OF WAFFLES!

7 + 2 + 2 + 3 + 4

I MUST ADMIT IT . . .
THIS IS ONE SWEET SUBJECT!
DELECTABLE!
DELICIOUS!
TASTY!
SCRUMPTIOUS!
DIVINE!
TOOTHSOME!
PALATABLE!
FLAVOURFUL!
YUMMY!

SCIENCE SQUAD

SQUAD

VS.

FUN
FINDERS

SO WHAT'S NEXT?

HOW ABOUT . . .

SCIENCE!

A FIELD TRIP!

WELL, IF WAFFLES PLUS MATHS EQUALS WAFFLEMATICS . . .

THEN HOW ABOUT . . .

A SCIENCE FIELD TRIP?

LET'S SPLIT INTO TWO TEAMS, SWIM AROUND AND SEARCH FOR AS MANY FASCINATING FACTS AS POSSIBLE!

TOTALLY!

OKAY!

SI!

ALRIGHT!

AYE! SURE!

FINS UP!

YES! OKEYDOKEY!

EACH TEAM CAN ASK A CREATURE ABOUT THEIR FEATURES! THEIR CAPABILITIES! WHAT THEY DO!

THE TEAM THAT DISCOVERS THE MOST FUN FACTS WILL WIN A WAFFLEY BIG SURPRISE!

WOO! HOO! HUZZAH! YAY!

HURRAH! HURRAY! YA!

YES! YIPPEE!

FINCH, FINNIE, DELFINA, FINNARD AND FINNEGAN . . .

YOU'RE WITH ME.

WE'LL MEET BACK HERE IN . . .

THIRTY-THREE MINUTES!

UM . . . OKAY! THIRTY-THREE MINUTES. GO!

swoosh!

swish!

FINTASTIC

FACT-FINDING
SCIENCE
SCAVENGER
HUNT!

LET'S EXPLORE!

SEEK!

SEARCH!

SURVEY!

INVESTIGATE!

THIS WAY!

DIRECTION!

PATH!

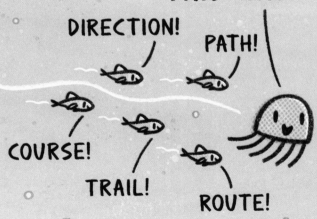

COURSE!

TRAIL!

ROUTE!

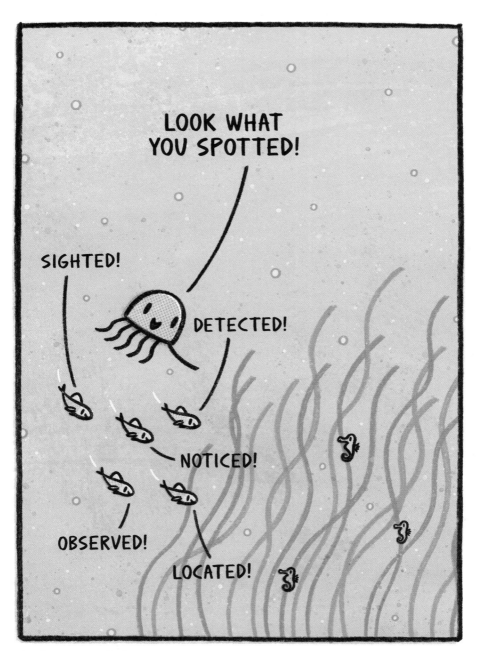

EXACTLY THIRTY-THREE MINUTES LATER . . .

THE RESULTS!

TEAM JELLY
A.K.A. SCIENCE SQUAD

① SEAHORSES ARE FISH!

② MALE SEAHORSES CAN GIVE BIRTH TO MORE THAN 1,000 BABIES AT ONCE!

I'M A DAD WHO DELIVERS!

③ BABY SEAHORSES ARE CALLED FRY.

④ SEAHORSES CAN CHANGE COLOUR!

TEAM NARWHAL
A.K.A. FUN FINDERS

① THERE ARE 22 SPECIES OF ALBATROSS.

② THE WINGSPAN OF THE WANDERING ALBATROSS CAN REACH UP TO 12 FEET— OVER 3.5 METRES!

③ THEY CAN FLY AS MUCH AS 10,000 MILES (ABOUT 16,000 KM) IN ONE GO.

> I'VE GOT A LOT OF SKY MILES!

④ THEY CAN LIVE 50+ YEARS!

⑤ THEY CAN FLY OVER 50 mph (ABOUT 80 km/h)!

BUT WE HAVE A PROBLEM.

A PROBLEM?

ANOTHER WAFFLE-MATICS PROBLEM!

HOW DO WE DIVIDE THIS WAFFLE AMONG US ALL EQUALLY?

ALL OF US?

YEP! FOR SURE! THE BEST PRIZES ARE ONES YOU SHARE!

BESIDES, MY BELLY IS ALREADY
BURSTING FROM ALL THOSE
WAFFLES I ATE EARLIER!

hee! hee!

TAG!
YOU'RE
~~IT!~~
AWESOME!

TIME FOR BREAK!

YES!!!

HMMM, OKAY. I GUESS IT'S GOOD TO TAKE A BREAK . . .

BUT ONLY FOR A LITTLE BIT. WE SHOULD GET BACK TO LESSONS SOON.

TAG! YOU'RE IT!

hee! hee!

I'M WHAT?

IT!

PROFESSOR KNOWELL, HAVE YOU NOT PLAYED TAG BEFORE?

DO YOU MEAN ULTIMATE OCTOPUS TAG?

UH . . . NO. JUST REGULAR TAG.

IS THAT LIKE FLIPPER FREEZE TAG OR TURTLE TWIRL TAG?

ER, NO IDEA. IT'S JUST . . . TAG.

AND YOU'RE "IT".

BUT WHAT IS "IT"?

"IT" IS "IT"! AND YOU ARE I**T**!

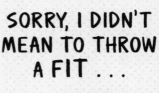

SORRY, I DIDN'T MEAN TO THROW A FIT . . .

I JUST DON'T GET WHY YOU DON'T GET IT.

ME NEITHER! THIS VERSION DOESN'T MAKE NEARLY AS MUCH SENSE AS SUPER SURF SWIRL TAG . . .

BUT I HAVE AN IDEA!

?

swish!

I AM? HUH!

IN THAT CASE . . .

TAG! YOU'RE COOL!
TAG! YOU'RE GREAT!
TAG! TAG! TAG!

FABULOUS!
MARVELLOUS!
WONDROUS!
TREMENDOUS!

YOU'RE REMARKABLE! RAD! EXTRAORDINARY! SPECTACULAR!

PANT, PANT
THAT WAS
FUN!

YOU GOT
EVERYONE!
JELLY, YOU
REALLY ARE
INCREDIBLE!

SUPER WAFFLE
AND <u>STRAWBERRY</u> SIDEKICK

VS.

The Mucus Monster

by

Professor Knowell, Jelly, Fin, Finneas,
Finnie, Finbar, Finley, Finnegan,
Delfina, Finch and Finnard

ONE DAY WHEN SUPER WAFFLE AND
STRAWBERRY SIDEKICK WERE HAVING A
BUBBLE BLOWING BATTLE . . .

EEK!

ICK!

ACK!

THEY WERE INTERRUPTED BY THE CRIES OF A BUNCH OF LITTLE FRIES. SOME CREATURE HAD EATEN THEIR TEACHER!

A MONSTER! A BEAST! A BEHEMOTH!

SUPER WAFFLE **AND** STRAWBERRY SIDEKICK

TO THE RESCUE!

IT APPEARS TO BE SOME SORT OF MUCUS MONSTER!

IT'S EEW-MONGOUS!

gurgle!

Snort! Snuff!

THIS ISSUE
REQUIRES TISSUES!

THIS SHOULD DO
THE TRICK TO GET
RID OF THE ICK!

LET'S WIPE THIS
BOOGER BEAST AWAY!

IT'S SNOT STOPPING!

squelch!
sniff!
slurp!

WE NEED A
SOLUTION . . . .

A BUBBLE
SOLUTION?

EAT SUDS, YOU SINISTER SLIME!

splurg...

IT'S DEFEAT-A-BUBBLE!

UNDER ALL THAT SNOTTY SCUM, SUPER WAFFLE AND STRAWBERRY SIDEKICK FIND MR. PINEAPPLE, THE TEACHER!

sniff!

MR. PINEAPPLE IS ILL-PREPARED TO TEACH TODAY.

I THINK I BEST GO GET SOME REST . . .

AND SO SUPER WAFFLE AND STRAWBERRY SIDEKICK FIND THEMSELVES SUBSTITUTE TEACHING . . .

THAT'S IT!
YOU'LL FRY-TEN YOUR FOES FOR SURE!

Ahoy, Mr. Blowfish!
We hope you'll enjoy/like/ appreciate this comic and these warm waffles! Feel better/well/healthy/ strong/great soon!

Best fishes!

Professor Knowell aka Narwhal, Jelly, Fin, Finneas, Finnie, Finbar, Finley, Finnegan, Delfina, Finch and Finnard

GOT SOME SNAIL MAIL FOR MR. BLOWFISH.

I'M ALWAYS HAPPY TO MAKE A SPEEDY DELIVERY!

AND FOR OUR NEXT LESSON —

EXCUSE ME, PROFESSOR KNOWELL . . .

SORRY!

PARDON!

BUT . . .

HOWEVER!

IT'S TIME . . .

THE HOUR . . .

TO GO . . .

JET . . .

OH! IT'S TIME TO GO?

HOW IS IT ALREADY SO LATE?! THERE'S STILL SO MUCH TO LEARN!

LIKE . . . UNDERWATER BASKET WEAVING AND —

MUSIC, GEOGRAPHY, GRAMMAR AND HISTORY . . .

OR TOMORROW YOU CAN TEACH US! MAYBE SYNCHRONISED SWIMMING!

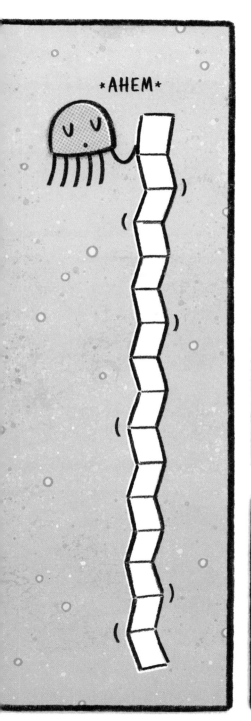

W!

WAIT. WHAT'S A "W" MEAN?

A "W" IS FOR WAFFLES! BECAUSE WAFFLES ARE FUN, SWEET, AWESOME AND UNIQUE.

JUST LIKE YOU! AND YOUR TEACHING TOO! ACTUALLY, HOW ABOUT A "W+" 'CAUSE YOU'RE . . .

ALL THOSE THINGS PLUS MORE!

WOW! A "W+"! THANKS, JELLY!

I THINK THIS CALLS FOR ONE LAST ROUND OF . . .